B
CO

C000319011

DIALECT

A Selection of Words and Anecdotes
from the Black Country

By
Brendan Hawthorne

BRADWELL
BOOKS

Published by Bradwell Books
Carrwood Road, Chesterfield S41 9QB
Email: info@bradwellbooks.co.uk

The right of Brendan Hawthorne as author of this work
has been asserted by him in accordance
with the Copyright, Design and Patents Act, 1988.
All rights reserved. No part of this publication
may be produced, stored in a retrieval system or transmitted
in any form or by any means,
electronic, mechanical, photocopying, recording or
otherwise without the prior permission of
Bradwell Books.

British Library Cataloguing in Publication Data: a catalogue
record for this book is available
from the British Library.

1st Edition

ISBN: 9781902674513

Print: CPI Group (UK) Ltd, Croydon, CR0 4YY

Design by: JenksDesign

Photograph Credits: Brendan Hawthorne & Sandwell
Community History & Archives Service

INTRODUCTION

To this day, I continue to discover more about the Black Country's rich heritage of language and stories, despite being born in the region in the early sixties and living here ever since.

Perhaps this is what has inspired my fascination for the oral traditions of the language and anecdotes of my home region. It's probably also why, after a hands-on education as a factory electrician, I now 'work with words' as a freelance writer, songwriter and performance poet.

As I hope you'll discover within these pages, the dialect of the Black Country is as steeped in history as its landscape and as packed full of character as its people.

The stories I share in this book reveal just how much the places and the people of the Black Country have been through - from boom to bust to, hopefully, reinvention. Now that its canal networks and industrial archaeology are fast becoming popular tourist attractions, it looks like the richness of the Black Country is being discovered afresh.

I hope that you too will enjoy discovering the Black Country through its fascinating dialect. Make yourself 'at wum'!

Brendan Hawthorne 2013

A

Abed - in bed, not got up yet

Abrawd - in foreign climes

Aer - our

Aerche - (erk) ache

Aerdew - hello

Aerren - (air en) either one

Afower - before

Agin - again

Aginst - against

Allus - always

Anunst - against

Ar - I

Atin - eating

Ay - not, as in in it *ay* that 'un

Aydedaydy - person who is half-soaked

B

Babby - baby

Baercon - bacon

Baersun - basin, as in sugar basin

Bally - stomach

Bally-aerchin - complaining

B

Balm pot - foolish, a silly person

Bawling - shouting

Bay - not

Baywindered - posh

Bibble - a rounded stone

Bin - are

Bisn't - am not

Bist - am

Black Bats - collective slang for large beetles

Blart - sob, cry childishly

Blooms - iron ore

Bobonyerself - think highly of yourself

Bogole - cellar

Bonk - hill

Bost - broken

Bostin - great, really good

Brassick lint - skint, no money

Brassy - cocky, full of self

Brawd - common

Brekfuss - breakfast

Brew'uss - brew house, outbuilding

Brum - Birmingham, home of white metal industries
(silver and pewter)

Brummy - person from Birmingham

B

Bunfyer - bonfire, outdoor fire

Butty - a mine owner or manager, a type of canal boat

Buzz - bus, passenger carrying vehicle

C

Caerk - cake

Caerkole - mouth

Caff - café or local greasy spoon

Caggy - left, as in left-handed

Cadge - to borrow or be given

Cant - talk or gossip

Catlick - very quick wash

Chap - boy/young fellow, mate

Chappin - girls looking for boys to court

Cheyer - chair

Chimdey - chimney

Chincuff - bad cough

Chittlins - meal made from animal intestine

Chops - cheeks

Chuck - throw

Chunter - grumble

Churchyard cuff - consumption or bronchitis

Clack - throat or group of friends

C

Clammed - starving, hungry

Clane - clean

Clunch - flaky soil often waste from a pit and containing ironstone

Cock - the top dog/best fighter

Cockaiver - a big hit, usually with a hammer

Codge - make a mess of things

Coolers - cooling towers, power station

Coot - courting as in courting couple

Cor/Cort/Cosn't - can't

Costive - constipation

Cracker - limestone refining process, sound of machinery

Crips - crisps

Cuff - cough

Cuss - swear, moan or tell off

Cut - canal

Cut off 'n' play - leave me alone

D

Daerty 'arfcrown - lady of the night

Darecent - dare not

Daycent - decent

Diper - sanitary towel

D

Dobbeninnet - being reported for doing something

Dollop - serving or pile

Dolly - used for washing clothes

Dost - did

Dower - door

Drap - drop

Dun - done

E

Entry - passageway between houses

Essole - ashcan or flue in a fireplace

Eyam/eyare - here you are

E'yar/e'yowam - here you are

F

Faerce - face

Faerke - cigarette

Faerther - father

Faet - feet

Faggits - faggots, food similar to haggis

Fettled - dressed

Finicky - fussy, in particular to food

F

Fittle - food

Fizzog - face

Floower - floor

Fode - courtyard/area at back of house

Fortnit - fortnight, two weeks

Forrid - forehead

Fossuck - to find out, prospect for

Frangy - tetchy, moody

Frisk - slag heap

Frit - frightened

Froz - frozen or cold

Fun - found

Fust - first

Fyer - here

G

Gabbin' - mouthing off

Gaffer - manager, boss, head of house

Gain - fit for purpose, best thing for job

Gammy - dodgy, lame, gammy-legged

Gamp - brolly, umbrella

Ganzy - cardigan

Gawky - ungainly, awkward

G

Gawp - stare vacantly

Giy / Giz - give

Glede - a glowing nugget of coal

Glory 'ole - furnace

Goo - go

Gob - mouth

Gobbing - spitting

Gorrabobontheself - high opinion of self

Graert - good; or part of fireplace

Graize - scuff the skin

Granfaerther - grandad

Granmutha - grandmother

Graunch - grind bones or teeth

Grorty - groaty pudding, grorty dick

Gummy - person with no teeth

Guzzunder - pee pot (goes under bed)

H

Hailstone - roadstone that was quarried by blasting - sounded like hail as it landed

I

Injin - engine
Irons - cutlery
Izzen - belonging to him

J

Jack-bannock - stickleback, small fish
Jed - dead
Jeff - deaf
Jerkin - waistcoat
Jerry - chamber, pee-pot
Jerrycan - tea can used in factories
Jeth - death

K

Kay - key
Kaylied - drunk
Ketch - catch
Kisser - lips, mouth

L

Lampin - beating up, gid a gud lampin

Lather - worked up, all of a lather

Lezzer - meadow

Licker - hot pork fat, bread dip from lard

Lights - lungs or the lungs of an animal - food

Loff - laugh

Lugole - ear

Lummux - clumsy, ungainly person

M

Maidintub - tub used for clothes washing

Marlole - disused clay pit filled with water

Mate - meat

Maygrum - facial expression of distaste

Mek - face

Mettle - strength, toughness

Midden - tip, place for waste

Mitha - to keep questioning, fretful

Mizzle - fine rain

Mollycoddled - fussed over, spoiled

Mon - man

Mongas - type of gas from coal

Monondled - treated roughly

M

Mooch/moach - search
Mowta - motorcar
Mucker - friend
Mush - mouth or friend
Mutha - mother

N

Naerber - neighbour
Naerren - neither one
Napper - head
Nightsilemen - midden cleaners
Nitnuss - school nurse
Noddleyead - foolish person
Noggin - chunk of thick bread
Nogyead - slow thinker
Noshers - teeth, usually false
Nowse - inteligence, guile
Nowt - nothing
Nuss - nurse

O

Ockered - awkward
Ommer - hammer
Ond - hand
Ooman - woman
Opples - opples
Oss rowd - road or street
Otch - move – 'otch up a bit'
Owamya? - how are you?
Owd - old

P

Packin - stodgy food
Palin - beating up or upright part of fence
Passnip - parsnip
Pays - peas
Pelmet - fringed trim over window
Penickety - fussy
Perler - fall – 'went a right perler'
Piece o bread - sandwich
Plaerte - plate
Pluck - offal
Po - chamber pot
Podge - poke or push in

P

Podger - rug-making stick or a queue-jumper
Pon - pan
Prial - three, three of same card
Privvy - usually describes an outdoor toilet of single occupancy
Puck - pick
Puddled - confused, not all the ticket
Puss - purse

Q

Quid (note) - pound in money

R

Raerker - large piece of coal
Rag mon - scrap dealer, 'tat mon'
Reesty - dirty, infested
Rodney - dirty, idle, poor
Rot - rat
Rottin - sport of rat catching

S

Saft - stupid

Sate - seat, seat of chair

Scrap - waste metal or a fight

Shaps - shops

Sharra - coach

Sheed - shed (as a tree sheds leaves)

Shek - shake

Shert - shirt

Shewez – shoes

Shyed - throw – use as in coconut shy

Skewel – school

Skilly - watery thin porridge or soup

Skint - without money

Skweej - squeeze

Snap - food, packed lunch

Snoggin - kissing

Snoz - nose

Spake - speak

Sparrer - sparrow

Spitting - used with wind-blown rain

Squab - cushion or soft seating

Squayell - squeal

Squilt - spot or blackhead

Stiffket/sustiffket - certificate

S

Stond - stand

Stoon - stone

Suck - sweets, confectionary

Suff - lower part of chimney/fireplace – 'chuck it up the suff', throw it away

T

T'/Th' - prefix vowel to mean 'the'

Taerters - potatoes

Tarrarabit - bye for now

Tat - scrap

Tay - tea as in cup of or meal

Tek - take

Terrar - bye

Thining cap on - in thought

Thissen - this one

Thother - the other

Thotherun - the other one

Thowd mon - father or husband

Tittle-tattle - tell tales or gossip

Tocky - sticky clay soil

Traerpsin - aimlessly walking

Tranklements - ornaments, personal belongings

T

Trotters - type of horse or pigs feet
Tunky - portly, fat

U

Um - home
Upthestick - pregnant

V

Varmint - a rogue or someone who is playfully naughty
Vessy - vest

W

Waggin - truant, not at work
Wammel - dog of many breeds
Wazzin - back of throat
Weej - which
We'em - we are
Weersyagooin? - where's he going?
Welly - effort
Wenchin - men seeking to court a lady
Werk - work

W

Werk 'uss - work house

Werrit - fret or worry

Wick - period of one week/nerves

Wickend - weekend

Winda - window

Woe - won't

Woolest? - will you?

Wum - home

Wust - worst or will you?

Y

Yam yam - person from Black Country

Yampy - mad or eccentric

Yed - head

Yo/Ya - you

Yo bay bist? - you're not are you?

Numbers

Wun/un - one	Fust - first
Tew - two	Secunden - second
Threey - three	Therdun - third
Fower - four	Fowerthun - fourth
Foive - five	Fifthun - fifth
Sicks - six	Sixthun - six
Sevun - seven	Seventhun - seventh
Aett - eight	Aerthun - eighth
Nyenne - nine	Nyennthun - ninth
Ten - ten	Tenthun- tenth

Conversational Black Country

Please remember when speaking in Black Country it is usual to make very long sentences so that they all run together to make one long breathless word that can sound incredibly confusing to the untrained ear! Phew!

Aerdew aer kid, aer bin ya?
Hello my friend how are you?

Well blow me darn with a rag mons trumpet
A term used to express surprise and awe

Yo'm gerrin on ma wick yo am nah goo an cut off an play
You're getting on my nerves you are now get out of my
sight

Yo bayn't a bad un bisn't?
You're not a bad one are you?

Lends yower faerce ter goo rottin
A term used to comment upon how someone looks

Gorra faerce like a fightin cock
A term used to describe someone flushed with temper

Keep ahrt th'oss rowd
Keep out of the horse road, stay safe

'E couldn't stop a pig in entry
Description of someone who is bow-legged

I'll shove this under yer loffer
An offering of an uppercut to the chin

Ahrm from ……..Strong in the arm an saft in the yed
A Black Country term prefixed by the town of someones
birth to describe their finer points!

Yo think on
I don't forget

In the nuddy
Naked

It's a bit black over Bill's mother's
It's looking like rain (Bill in this case is Kaiser Bill – Kaiser
Wilhelm II of Germany and refers to bad weather usually
coming from an north easterly direction, though it can
mean bad weather from wherever is imminent!)

Any road up – either way

Introduction

The Black Country is a land-locked region that covers the heartland of England, its geological make up and geographical position contributing, during the Industrial Revolution, to its reputation as the Workshop of the World.

Farming and pottery industries gave way to the demands of the modern world. New processes in manufacturing and production demanded vast quantities of iron and coal to feed voracious furnaces and order books. The Black Country had, what must have seemed like a limitless quantities of iron and coal beneath its cankered skin.

Canals were cut, criss-crossing the rapidly changing landscape and formed the superhighways of transport before rail and road finally caught up. In fact the Black Country town of Tipton was reported to have more miles of canal than Venice! We also have the infamous River Tame meandering its' way across the region. Its' natural course is mainly underground but where it rises it has often had its course changed by the needs of man and machine. The river is much cleaner today but in the past due to pollution, soil make up and other detritus it became known locally as 'The Black Brook'.

The region became home to generations of itinerant workers bringing tales, words and phrases from the broader isles. However, the core of the Black Country dialect was forged and is firmly rooted in the Anglo-Saxon languages that came to this area in the tenth century. It is still regarded today as one of the oldest and purest forms of Middle English. Its speech patterns, word order, and in some cases, the words themselves have remained relatively unchanged by the pressures of an ever shifting identity in language. The strength of dialect and language is partly due to generations of indigenous people not having to leave the area to find work.

Each area of the Black Country has its own distinct dialect both in how it sounds and how it's written. The sing-along Dudley dialects give way to the flatter sounds of Tipton and Wednesbury and the more nasal and guttural sounds of the surrounding areas. In some areas of the Black Country you can literally cross the 'oss road for a completely different sounding dialect.

Much of what follows is taken from personal accounts and presents a warts and all picture of growing up in the area, its influences and foibles through the post war baby boomer years. It reflects on good times, bad times and how the spirit of the region has survived through some very difficult times

Quarry trucks at Rowley

of austerity and deprivation whilst still maintaining core traditions of language, culture and friendliness. It will be noted that anecdotes are set in a very specific area of the Black Country as all are taken from personal experience with a touch of poetic licence!

The region, on the whole, is a vibrant and diverse area where positives have always seemed to outweigh the negatives through the can-do spirit of this heartland and I, like many others, are proud to say that they are Black Country born and bred!

This little book also offers a beginners guide to the rich and varied language of a wonderfully diverse and often overlooked region of England.

Just think on it. Even owd Billy Shaerkespeare 'd a spoke laerk we'en do eya an e wort even frum these parts!

A fine welcome!
The Black Country prides itself on making people welcome to its hearth and home. Over the years it has had its industry but has held very little wealth for working families. The only way a family could share hospitality was to keep a scrubbed front door step, clean windows and provide food on their tables for family and friends. You could always tell when you were welcome and most definitely when you were not!

Terraced and courtyard housing stock.
Much of it still in existence today.

A work mate went to visit a colleague who was 'on the box' (off sick). He walked up to the door of his mate's house and rang the bell. His owd mucker answered and ushered him in. 'Aer bin ya owd un?' asked the visitor with concern. 'arm a dooin awright, dost thee want a cuppa an a piece o caerke?' Came the reply. 'Are that'd be graert, con thee manage?' offered the visitor. 'Yow sit the're un aerl be back in a bit', fended the patient.

The visitor sat down and started to look around him just as the patient's pet dog came in to check out the disturbance. The patient shuffled in behind with a piece of cake and neatly presented it to his visitor on a white crock plate.

'Eyer's yer caerk an I'll fetch yer tay now'. 'Ta maerty am yo sure yo'm ok?' 'Aer I bin aer' loffed the patient.

Just on it the dog, who had shown no real interest up until this point, sat at the visitor's feet and started growling and barking. With a mouthful of cake the visitor asked, 'What's the marrer wi yower dog owd pal? Doe e like me or summat?' 'Nah 'e's awright' said the patient handing over a mug of tea, 'He's allus like that.' 'Wot yo mean allus like that?' asked visitor warily. 'E's allus like that when someone's atin off 'is plaerte!' came the shocking reply!

Welcomes were also extended to new workers in factories. My grandfather worked as a glassblower and blew industrial standard glass for Stevens and Williams. On the platform, the lead hand blew each glass item and then handed the job over to the rest of his gang for finishing off. That's where me granfaerther held court. He'd re-heat his fatty baercon sandwiches at the side of the 'glory 'ole' on every shift. He took pride in his work and became highly regarded for his skills and teaching abilities. He was a keen piece worker. That meant when he had blown his quota of glass for the day he'd be off down the pub before his shift time had ended to replenish the bodily fluids he'd sweat out in front of the furnace. However, sometimes he would be delayed through no fault of his own. Sometimes when handing over his work his team maertes would drop or damage the item intended for finishing. Eyewitnesses have told me that he would say very little to them but would wait for them to stand up from their workplace bench to go and ansa a call of naerture. In their absence he would get some hot metal (molten glass) on the end of a blowing iron and sprinkle it on the sacking were the offender sat. When they returned and sat down they would unknowingly set their own arse alight! Many a mon has bin sin ajumpen araernd dowsing his smouldering moleskin trowsers. Interestingly they were much more careful in receiving glass from me granfaerther and they rarely re-offended!

Christmas time was allus med special with me granfaerther bringing 'end of day glass' baubles home, frosted in glass powder and ready to hang on the tree with a match tail and piece of string. The rest of the year would be celebrated with glass swans and other ornaments and

Stevens and Williams lead glassblower Sam Hickinbottom
blowing what appears to be 'bull's eye' glass for windows in
February 1956

trinkets. You could always tell when my grandfather was
home. You'd hear his feet first clod-'opping up th'entry in his
work boots and then you'd smell his overcoot that would still
be smouldering from a carelessly snipped Park Drive cigarette
that he'd put in his pocket before walking into aer um.

Where yo frum?

People from this area are often confused with being
Australian even though we don't have end of sentence
inflexions. However, people from the coal and steel industries

of South Wales can often tell which town in the Black Country you're from due to industrial connections through transport networks.

Several years ago at a meeting in the old Black Country town of Tipton an idea was presented to a longstanding committee regarding a new history/community project. Unfortunately for the manager of the project a bristling sense of belonging was soon established amongst the participants. Many towns still have a village or parochial identity that can cause irritation to outsiders who wish to impart their will and wisdom. The meeting went something like this and is more than likely echoed across many towns and situations in this region:

Manager of proposed project – We will of course be able to bring this service to you and we think it will have a positive impact on your community and also be a lasting legacy for future generations

Community representative – Eya we am agen. Some aertsiders comin in atellin we wot we want. Why doe yer ask we instead of assuming we cort think fer we selves? There's a lot o good people eya purra lot o ard werk in ter doin things n get no thanks n yo lot just waltz in eya an tek over proceedings

Manager of proposed project –I'm not an outsider, I'm from the area myself

(At this point I have to add that the project manager was now walking on very thin ice!)

Community representative – Weya yow frum then if yo say yo'm frum these parts?

Manager of proposed project – I'm from just the other side of Walsall

Community representative – That ay frum rarnd eya though is ett? And while we'm on (turning to me) where am yo frum?

(I thought I was on on safe ground here as Tipton is my home town)

Me – I'm frum Tip'on

Community representative – Ar that's good but which part?!

Pig iron removal

Payday

Payday in industry was usually on a Thursday (except when it wuz Saturdays!) so that any discrepancies could be sorted out on Friday (except when it wuz Saturdays!) Money was very tight and the menfolk would see it as a right to goo to the alehouse fust before tekking their hard earned money um to wife and kids. This would often lead to the wage queues on one side of the factory fence being exchanged for queues of women on the other side of the factory fence as they attempted to get to their husbands' wages first!

Colliery winding

Beliefs and superstitions

As in moost areas of the country there are a lot of general superstitions. One area of industry known fer its culture of superstitions relates directly to mines and the safety of the miners 'emselves. A list uv superstitions was found over the mantle of a fireplaerce at an owd Black Country inn. Here's a version of the list converted into aer dialect!

Doe yo ever goo ter the pit if yo've dreamt of a broken clog or a fire or if the raerker yo put in the graert the night before is unlit the morning afore yower shift they'm sure signs o daernger. If yo meet an ooman at dawn on the way to the pit goo back um: it's a sure sign o death else. When yo get ter the pit an yo see bright lights in the mine turn as quick as a whimsy n run as fast as yo con. If yo 'ear howling it's Gabriel's hell hounds so turn around and doe do any werk that day. If yo smell a foul stink at pit it's a sign that imps have bin at play so turn abahrt and goo um fer yer own saerfty. If yo want ter damn the evil spirits tek a bible an kay in yer right ond and say the Lords Prayer: that'll send em on their way.

Pastimes

Living in an industrialised area allows you to see another type of poetic beauty that is less obvious than in more rural settings. There were the dangers of marl 'oles. Those deep straight sided clay pits that had become filled with water, a by product of the blue and red brick industries that pock-marked the area. There were many brick companies including the Darlaston Brick Company and Blades Bricks. I grew up darn the road from the marl 'ole an in the shadder of Ocker Hill power station. It was where me graert granfaerther werked on the turbines. Those three mossive coolers produced plumes ov steam that sometimes eclipsed the sun. In me early years I believed that the power staertion was a cloud factory and I would shout at it on a summer's day fer blockin the sun. Other times I'd be mesmerised by the constant stream of straernge 'n' mythical cloud shaerpes. The

Doulton Kiln, Rowley Regis

neighbourhood would be covered in grit and outfall but at least we knew we had th'electric.

When I was a kid mah playgraernd wuz the local canals. We'd spend ages running along tow paths, seeing cootin couples snoggin under bridges. We'd build ramps fer we bikes to jump on an' skiff stoons over the stagnant cut waerter green wi scum tekkin care not to fall in. There was an owd sayin that went like 'It ay what yo fall in with it's what yo climb out with uz wot counts!'

Dominating the landscape. Two of the three cooling towers at
Ocker Hill power station and a tropical fish enclave!

Apart from the industrial slurry, dead animals and rats, the
canal was full of booty. Owd bikes, bedsteads, motorscooters
etc. Sometimes if yo wuz lucky yo'd find what looked like an
owd nut. It was the leather money puss o one th' owd werkers
that ad got all cankered up in the waerter an sometimes
there'd be coin in em. One day though dahrn by the warm
waerter outfall from the power staertion cooling towers we
sid a sight. We woz used ter seein jack bannocks or the odd
carp in the murky waerter but this day we wuz agog wi
excitement. For there in the cut was tropical fish! Somebody
had emptied their tank, musta got fed up wi em, into the cut

38

Locks at Tipton

by the warm waerter that stood abahrt seventy degrees Fahrenheit. Fer months we'd goo darn n feed um until the winter finally took em when the waerter temperature drapped. Now that was true excitement!

Marleys and fobbers

A marley, or marble, was used in the many variants of traditional marble street games whether they were from the top of a pop bottle or the gloriously coloured glass ones. A fobber was a larger marble and usually took two strikes to win. The true treasure was a steely. It was a ball bearing

Mayday birth of Socialism

probably taken from a machine bearing. Great if your mom or dad worked in tool setting or machine shops!

I remember one of ma maertes producing a steely that was as big as an 'opple. He declared proudly 'This is a fiftier!' Meaning it took fifty winning strikes to take it from him. Regardless to say no-one won it but he took plenty of our marbles in the many vain attempts we had in trying to obtain it!

Street Gaermes

Moost street gaermes were med up of what could be found in the street or on the waste grounds and demolition sites in the neighbourhood. It will be quite obvious to the reader that health and safety was not a priority when some of these games were popular!

A skipping rhyme follows of unknown origin but is one part of many variants taken from a traditional English folk song called The Cuckoo Song:

The cuckew's a pretty baerd
'er singeth as 'er flies
'er flits across the medder
'er telleth we no lies

Tip Cat

Items needed:

A pebble

A wooden clothes peg

A large wooden stick or branch to use as a bat

Plaerce a cloos peg on a bibble wi its 'ead or prongs overhanging th' edge. Bring a boster of a stick darn on th' overhanging side o' the cloos peg to flick the peg inter the air and send it spinning. While the cloos peg is in the air the batsmon lamps the peg wi' a right cockaiver. The winner is 'im uz could send the peg the farest.

Fire Can

Items needed:

Tin can

length of string

kindling

matches

Gerra can an' tie sum string or wire to ett. Stuff ett wi' paerper an' wood un set it alight. Swing the can araernd thee napper an' create a roaring sound.

Aunt Sally

Items needed:

Ten (or however many sticks could be found) sticks that could be stood on end or use skittles

A stick for chucking

Arraernge the skittles in a row or in rows. Chuck the stick to knock down the skittles. The winner is the person who could knock down the moost skittles

Stick and hoop

Items needed:

one stick

one hoop from a cask or barrel

Plaerce the 'oop on its edge on edge an roll ett wi' the stick. Chaerce it up an darn th'oss bonks fer as long as yo con!

Then, of course, there wuz the funfair an' circuses at the waerkes. These were usually Bank Holiday celebrations when the travellers and showmen come ter town and laid on amusements at the local green spaerces

Outin' on the chara'

Gud 'ealth an 'umour

The Black Country dialect has lent itself to some jokes in itself. The pronunciation of some words allows a bending of the issue in hand, the old joke of 'Kipper tie?' sounding like 'cuppa tea?' for instance. One old bloke in a pub raised his glass to the health of his mate and shouted 'Chayers!' meaning 'Cheers!' His mate drunkenly replied ''n taerbles ter yo an all wi knobs on!'

And so to a story so true it couldn't be fictional!

A maert o' mine had bin sufferin' from ill 'ealth an' went ter see 'is docta. The docta purrim on some different tablets, red uns ar think, an asked im ter see ow 'e gorron. Well…. after a fortnit me maerte went ter see 'is docta ter tell 'im ow 'e wuz a doin'. How are you keeping?' the docta asked in a posh tone (musta bin from Greart Barr or somewhere like that). Me maert replied 'I aysa bad generally spakin'. The docta continued 'is line o' questioning, 'Any side effects?' 'Loike wot?' me maerte replied ''cos if ar doe know wot they bin ar cort tell ya con I?' Well, the docta continued unerred, 'Have you had any problems (ahem) with erections?' 'Nah!' me maerte countered assuredly, 'Norratall. Ar mean ar purra gazebo up last wik!'

Free enterprise

I wuz awalken um frum skewel wun day wi me maertes an sid an owd pick up truck struggling ter gerrup th'll we wuz walken up. It wuz a clapped ahrt owd knackera n wuz lowded up wi scrap metal. Just as they passed us th'axle bost on the waggon 'n' that's when the polis sirens were heard. The tew dowers flung open an three blokes shot ahrt n set off in as

Horse-drawn at Holloway Bank

many directions. Well the next day in the paerper the story unfolded o these enterprisen blokes. They'd bin scrap collectin all day un depositin it at the local steelwerks. On their twelvth visit the bloke on the gaert said to um 'Yow've gorra gud supply ay yer?' to which the scrap blokes said 'Ar we 'ave n ther's plenty mower where this come from.' It dawned on the gaertmon then that they'd bin drivin rarnd the back on 'is werks an lowdin up from the back o the pile ter sell it 'im back rarnd the front!

Mindin yer pays an q's

In the Black Country the 'H' is silent at the start of most words beginning with 'H'! The trouble starts when a Black Country person tries ter spake posh or actin' above their staershun as we say around here. That's when all the H's are dropped and picked up randomly! At a posh dinner someone was overheard to say when complaining about undercooked vegetables.

'These pays haren't 'alf 'ard, I costn't bost 'em!'

Pigeon flying

Pigeon flying has always been very important to the Black Country. It involves a lot of expenditure by those taking part as well as total commitment to the well-being of the birds. It involves time spent in pubs and clubs at meetings and of course the excitement and disappointment of race days. The following was a conversation held by two old workmates on a Monday morning talking a bout the weekend and in particular the homing pigeon race.

Non pigeon fancier - Ahrd yower baerds gerron the wikend?

Pigeon fancier - Doe ask. I shud think they'm catchen the bus wum

Non pigeon fancier - Praps yo shud gerrem a bus pass that'd saerve yo the bus fayre

Pigeon fancier - They'n gorrit when they come wum. They ay wuth the corn so I'm pullin the necks They'm gooin in the bin

Non pigeon fancier - Yo cor do thet. Thet's cruel. I adn't got yo darn as a cruel bloke

Pigeon fancier - I ay cruel. It's a quick end if they ay no good. I cort afford ter keep keep em an it's a better end than 'em gerrin injured and dyin slow

Non pigeon fancier - Is thet right? Yo'm on'y killen 'em cos they ay quick enough. Tay their fault

Pigeon fancier - That's wot I'n allus dun since ar wuz a kid

Non pigeon fancier - Well instead o killen em why cort yo tek em somewhere nice that they doe know and just let 'em goo?

Pigeon fancier - !!!!!!!!!!!!!!!!!!!!!!!!!!

Cock fighting

Cockfighting had been a blood sport until it was outlawed in England and Wales in 1835. However, in its heyday all walks of life supported the so-called sport. An infamous traditional folksong 'Wedgbury Cocking' tells the story of the cockfights in Wednesbury held at 'The Olde Blue Ball Inn' where remnants of the pit can still be seen today. In its day the pub was locally known as 'Spittles' and had close geographical connections to the church on the hill. Local stories tell of 'runners' spreading the word that a fight was on and if one particular vicar was delivering a sermon he would be given a wink from the back of the church. The speed of the sermon would pick up so that he could finish and attend the fight as soon as possible. Some of the churchgoers might have been relieved if the sermon was dragging on a bit!

Gamecocks, or fighting cocks as they were called were fitted with metal spurs and combs. The fight was violent, bloody, gory and to the death. Money changed hands and fights often broke out between the spectators. Although regarded as a predominantly 'male' spectator sport, women also attended. Some of the men who had lost their money and drunk the rest would have to face their wives at home. Their wives all ruddied and angry would probably greet them with 'a faerce as red as a fightin' cock!'

Moosic

Befower the emergence of popular culture and local rock bands (Slade et al.) exporting even more heavy metal from the region there was the culture of dance. 'Ang onnabit though, let's digress a bit. In fact if yo recall Slade records in the days o vinyl yo ad Black Country spellin on the laerbels. Noddy the singer wi Slade also provides the lift announcements in Walsall's new art gallery. If yo want ter ear a Walsall accent goo an ride in the lift a bit. Best see the art work an all though!

Any road up, from the turn of the twentieth century up to the nineteen sixties live dance band moosic was very popular. Ballrooms and town halls held reglar dances an' gid extra work to part time moosicians. Me granfaerther, Sam Hickinbottom, was one uv these 'moosicians'. He played lead violin in Harold Stanton's Ballroom Dance Band. His missus played piano and youngest daughter (Glenys Raynor – The Pocket Soprano) sang operetta! The little owd terrace 'ouse that I spent my early years in would reglarly av dance band instruments and singers crowded into the tiny sitting room. All fed on cheese and onion cobs and jugs of beer! They med such beautiful moosic ter counter the steady grind of industry.

Live entertainment was a big thing at ballrooms and dance halls

Bare knuckle fighting

The Tipton Slasher was the most notorious of Black Country fighters. He was born in Tipton in 1819 and died in Wolverhampton in 1890. His training ground was at the Fountain Inn in Tipton and on the canalside shovelling coal where he wielded the broadest shovel to load coal onto the barges.

The fights were brutal with no limits on rounds. The sport encouraged gambling and attracted large prize pusses fer a gud scrap. William Perry, The Tipton Slasher, was Heavyweight Champion of England from 1850 – 1857 and was a well-respected figure in the community. There's a memorial to him in Coronation Gardens, Tipton.

Invention

During the fust bit o' the twentieth century a lot of industrial processes and breakthroughs occurred through hard werk an invention. It day stop though in the werld of industry. Folk wuz like ett at um, much ter do wi wimmen folk inventin ways o feedin families on low incomes.

Ma greart uncle was a bloke of invention. The shed which wuz situated at the back of the local pub (graert plaerce fer a shed!) wuz the um ov 'is radio transmitter. E built everything from scratch. All the crystal radios and amplifiers an he coated 'is own caerble and learned ter send an receive Morse

Code. A family story tells of how he wuz in contact wi somebody in Canada oo ad built their own radio transmitter. It just so happened that my great uncle was listening in for transmissions on a fateful night in 1912. He heard what could only be described as a faint distress signal but could not decipher it. It wasn't until the horror of the news that The Titanic had sunk did he realise what he had heard. Just over two years later he came home to find that the authorities had taken away his radio station. The outbreak of war had occurred and within a short space of time he became one of the many to lose their life in foreign fields. His job in the army? Frontline communications.

At werk

A factory once stood on a piece of land heading out towards the Black Country's northern borders of Wolverhampton. After close on a hundred and fifty years of manufacturing it was closed down and promptly turned into a housing estate or 'habitation corridor' as it said on the redevelopment plans. Any road up, when the factory was open it decided to replace a two mon job involving skill and precision into a one mon job. Basically ter purra mon with the use of his finger on the button of the new machine called a seam welder. Well they spent ages advertising for a seam welder operative and also searching out the right person for the job. The skilled job involved a plaerter with an 'ommer and taerpe measure and a welder joining steel plate together so that it could be turned into a liquid carrying container tank. The new post involved importing a huge machine that clamped the metal together and run a weld along it from an automated track. Excitement rose as the newly employed seam welder operative set foot on the shop floor and surveyed his new machine in front of a small and expectant crowd of management and fellow workers. The new bloke looked shocked, 'Wots this? I ay sid one o these afore, worrissit? I cort werk that'. The crowd shuffled its feet and a few managerial faces reddened until one manager broke the uneasy silence. "Yo said yo'ad nine 'ears experience seam weldin' so wots the problem?' 'Ar' said the new bloke, 'but that was on carrier bags not steel vessels!' Regardless to say the two blokes originally employed to seam weld continued their task until the new bloke had been given the necessary training.

Industry

Dudley, Oldbury, Tipton, Wednesbury and Bilston all had major steelworks that employed thousands of workers and took up huge swathes of land, their furnaces lighting the night skies like midnight suns. Over the region hung a smokestack pall blighting the Monday morning washing lines of many a household. Stories are told of one Dudley factory becoming the second home of one lady as she brought her washing in most Mondays to show the blight she had to face with her biled cotton. The said factory changed its manufacturing procedures to help keep the peace!

Smog over the Albion Works

Chain mekkin wuz a poorly paid and heavy job. A lot o the women folk med chain in small smithies as well as factories. They wuz paid be the yard. It wuz common plaerce fer an ooman ter gi' berth an wrap the new born babby up an plaerce close ter the furnace fer warmth whilst the 'er 'ud knock aert some mower lengths o chaern.

Limestone working was an important industry here. The stone went into the mettle of roads and buildings both as block and mortar but it also lined numerous furnaces. You

The New British Iron Company blast furnace

can still find 'marbleised limestone' on old slag heaps. The sound of the 'cracker' could be heard in many places. It was a process of heating limestone and then cooling it rapidly to crack the stone into smaller workable pieces.

Glass industries were a big part of the economy here in the Black Country. A lot of material was blown for domestic use as in ornaments and so forth with cut glass from Royal Brierley and Stevens and Williams. All of this sat alongside the enamelware of Bilston and the papier mache japanned wares of Wolverhampton! Walsall had its leather industries and coal was everywhere and could easily be picked from the surface as well as mined.

I had the pain and pleasure of working in a factry after leaving skewel. It taught me to have a sense of humour and that nothing in life was easy. The characters that existed in these environments gave you many views on life. Many times have the unsuspecting been sent to the stores for a long wait, a glass 'ommer or a sky hook.

One of the great rituals of factry life was being measured up for your overalls. It went summat like this.

'Yo want sum overalls then dun ya? Think yo'll like it 'ere then? Doe know whether yo'll a these afower we shut darn.

Owd yer arms ahrt then, mind me tay. Doe knock tharrover!' The man oos job it wuz shaerted out yer your measurements as he wrut 'em darn. He'd squint at his engineers taerpe measure. He would then tell you to 'waert a month for 'em to arrive' and when they did they felt like they were someone else's. It was on'y then yowed realise many of the overalls were the same size whether yo wuz six foot tall or five foot tall and whether yo ad the chest of an ox or a sparrer.

The one bit of fun we could have was making up names for the new receptionist to call out over the works tannoy. The dialect lent itself to making absurd names sound convincing. There are many names too blue or rude for this little volume but to give you an idea the unsuspecting lady would call out on our instruction 'Mr Know me, Joe Know me, 241please!' It pleased us so much then to shout back "No but we'd like to!'

Many factories also produced havens for wildlife. They often backed onto canal systems which had been left to nature to gerron wi' it. In fact the factory I worked at (some would argue 'attended'!) had a small meadow behind it. In winter the foxes would bring their young to the doors of the werkshaps where many a hard-bitten blue collar werker 'as gid up 'is brekfuss or dinner piece o bread ter feed the young uns. During the spring and summer months yo could walk

Lathe's Foundry, Tipton

through wild flowers sending a myriad of brightly coloured butterflies aflittin inter the air. It was allus times like that that med me realise how hand in hand wi naerture industry could be. The lot has gone now, bulldozed in the naerme of progress!

If yo look at some the naermes we got rarnd eya fer plaerces yo'll see the werd 'bloom' a lot. Areas such as 'Bloomfields' fer instance. Now the naerme sounds graert doe ett? All fields o flower blooms scentin the locals noses wi eavenly sniffs.

58

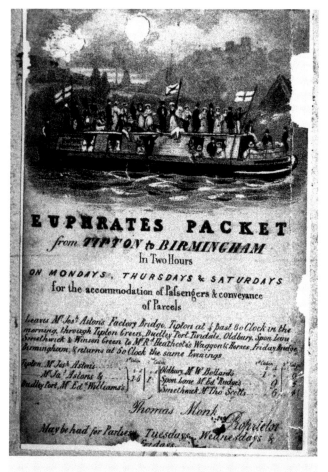

Monk's Steam Boat passenger carrying service

Unfortunately it couldn't be further frum the trewth. The werd 'bloom' or 'blom' as we also know ett derives frum the Anglo Saxon ter mean bloom but not entirely in a flower sense. Bloom is the naerme gid ter nodules of iron ore found in the area. The nodules resemble flower buds or flower heads and so the romantic sounding Bloomfields translaertes, mower or less, into fields of iron!

Canals

The industries of the Black Country were originally tethered together by canals. The link between low level Tipton and the hills of Dudley is a place called Dudley Port. It was where canals yielded to road and rail before being handed back to canal. Dudley Port was even considered to be a local beauty spot. A great uncle of mine took his new bride there for the day on their honeymoon, a round trip walk of some four miles!

Prior to engines being mounted on narrow boats they were initially towed or pulled by men and horses. Rope marks can be seen around many Black Country canal tunnels where ropes would bite into the cast iron and brickwork as horses pulled the boats through. Sometimes horses would be pushed to exhaustion and less scrupulous operators would be seen to light a fire under the osses arse to get it to stand up. This soon became an outlawed and shunned practice but the term lighting a fire under someone's arse is still remembered verbally as a way to let someone know that they are not pulling their weight.

Longer tunnels in Dudley had the crew 'leg the boat' This is where the crew would lie on their backs on top of the tarpaulined cargo and leg the boat through the tunnel by placing their booted feet on the inner walls of the tunnel and walking sideways to propel the boat. This was a very tiring procedure as one local tunnel is over three thousand yards in length!

Gerrin wot yo'n ask for

The art of communication is still an important aspect of getting things just right on both sides of a discussion. The following example of getting it wrong and making assumptions to justify the ends is one of the many true stories of Black Country wit, grit and loyalty.

Darn the caff

Two German businessmen went into a Black Country café and ordered a couple of English breakfasts to be accompanied by two lattes. The gentlemen paid for their fayre and went to find a seat. The fine fittle was to be produced fresh, hot and sizzling as only a good fry up should be. Within a matter of minutes two large plates of food

Three blokes darn the boozer. Singers and musicians enjoy a pint
at the local after work

arrived at the table with two industrial strength and sized teas
('builders' as it is known here). The German businessmen
looked puzzled as they thought they had clearly asked for
coffee - two lattes. A discussion ensued as to what should be
done next. Finally one of them got up and walked over to the
lady behind the counter and explained that he and his
colleague had ordered two lattes and clearly the content of
the mugs wasn't coffee. 'Ooh arr,' said the lady, 'Arm eversoo
sorry. Ar thought yo'n asked fer tew large tays!"

Heritage culture an pubs – music, comedy, beer

The traditional pub has gone into decline in these Isles over the last few years and this region is no different but there are still the gems of pubs offering light entertainment, open mic nights and so on in the area. The area has also had more than its fair share of breweries! Our humour has been portrayed in the comic strips of Aynuk and Ayli, two hapless blokes sharing a loff. We were home to the Black Country Night Out, a group of comics, musicians and poets who told taerls an loffed at the way we'en see things. Some of the notables here were bands like Giggetty, musicians like Jon Raven, comics like Dolly Allen and Tommy Mundon and poets like Jim William Jones.

The region has produced many comedians, actors and actresses, musicians, poets, writers, artists and sports people who have all gone on to national if not international status. Look 'em up, yowel be surprised!

Fittle Fit Fer A King ('an every werkin mon n ooman)

Even as late as the 1960's and 1970's meat or 'mate' as we know it in these parts was very definitely a luxury and only formed a small part of working class diets. Offal was often used as a substitute or cheap cuts of meat were biled fer owers until it wuz tender. Both of my grandmothers regularly had a stoowpot abiling all day ter feed the family at whatever time people med it um. My maternal grandmother however would

Tipton Butcher. A gud owd fashioned shap

turn savoury to sweet! She would slowly simmer a vegetable stew for an hour or so and then lower suet (beef suet, flour, water and seasoning) dumplings into it to make it go further and an fill yer clammed bally. For desert, the same beef suet would be biled fer tew owers or mower wi stoowed opple under neath in a cotton covered baersun tied wi string. The baersun 'ed rattle in a big pon of waerter an if it stopped rattlen yo knew it needed mower waerter. Then of course there wuz allus pork scratchins, black pudding an a piece of drippin'. No such luck wi' fat free!

Some of the old Black Country recipes are potentially stomach turning to read about but incredibly tasty, cheap and satisfying. The recipes are only to be regarded as an outline. Here are a few to look out for with some stories attached. These are most certainly not suitable for vegetarians!

Faggits an Pays (contents may vary)
Tek some pigs offal an fat, baercon rind and mince it darn ter a fine consitancy with sage and onion, flour, seazoning an other seazonal 'erbs and spices. Salt an peppa ter taerste. Tek the stummack linin o the pig and wrap rard a good 'ondfull o' the mince. Turn into balls ter fit in the palm o yer ond. Cook slowly in th'oven and mek gravy from any fat saerved b' the cookin process.

Grey pays shud be soaked fer a good twelve hours with alf crown size o bicarbonate of soda, rinsed an then biled when saft enuff ter squeej. The pays need ter be biled til they start ter goo mushy. Marrerfat pays con also be used.

Serve the faggits, when cooked, in a bowl (tew meks a bally bostin meal). Add a cupple servin spoons o pays an pour over the gravy. Add a noggin o bread. Yo might find the richness o this sustenance productive in bally gas. So warn yer friends an sleep wi the bedroom winder open and fer the sake o yer partner, preferably on yer own, unless of course, yo've both partaken and have an understanding and enduring relationship!

Me paternal grandmother lived in Ballfields, 'Ossley 'eath an on Thursdees it wuz 'arf day cloosin fer shaps an businesses so 'er'd be at the stove all day. The Belfast sink that looked out on the back fode ud be alive wi fresh eels waertin impershuntly ter be jellied an er'kitchen was stacked 'igh wi freshly cooked faggits that 'er'd plaert up with pays n graervy. Ahrd a me tay there on Thursdees after me schoolin 'ed finished cos that wuz family tradition. I'd stond an watch ahrt the front winder with mounting interest an hunger as the

Corn dealers

66

blokes off th'alottments stopped by wi loaded barrers o veg. 'Er'd be up an darn, up an darn openin the dower loaded up wi plaertes o fittle an then there 'er'd be. Me granmother'd swappin' them plaertes o steamin faggits an pays fer the payment of allotment food. It 'd keep 'er in veg fer until next Thursdee come abart. Wot con thee say abahrt ett but barterin at its best!

Grey Pays n Baercon

Get the fattiest barcon an cut inter strips, fry em off in lard an purrem in a large cookin pot wi plenty o waerter an soaked grey pays. Season ter suit an bile til thick. Serve wi a noggin a bread an follow the warnin fer faggits!

Grorty Dick (Groaty Pudding)

Put soaked grorts w (broken oats) wi mate (beef), add onions, leaks un stock an baerk em from morn til night in the middle oven. Shud be thick when served. Traditional on Bunfyer Night.

A friend and fellow poet of mine Geoff Stevens towd the story of an owd Black Country ooman oo was reknowned fer er Grorty Dick. They'd come from all over the plaerce just ter see ett. It wuz so stodgy and robust yo couldn't ate ett so 'er decided to improve the pointin on er outdower lavvy an that 'er did. 'Er trowled it in ter the gaps that the cowd wind blew through on a winter's mornen an finished the rest between the bricks. Trubble wuz when they come ter knock 'er 'ouse dahrn ett the times o the slum clearansen they put the wreckin ball on 'er house an it come darn pretty quick but do yo think they could shift that out dower privvy?

Stuffed sheeps hearts

Tek tew sheeps 'earts an an arnce o drippen, 'ondfull o' bread crums wi 'erbs un parsley. Add graerted lemon rind an a dessert spoom o' freshly chopped suet. Use a fresh chicken egg or milk ter bind.

A fruiterers on the road ter Wolvo

Wesh ther 'earts un cut ahrt the 'ard pipe wi' scissors. Soak the 'earts in tepid salt waerter fer twenty minutes or if yo'm inclined smoke a pipeful o' bacca whichever's longer. Rinse the 'earts in cowd waerter un dry off. Apart from the drippen mix all t'other ingredients together an' stuff the cavity o' the 'earts. Sew up th'openen an plaerce on a baerkin tray wi drippen on top o' th'earts. Cook on the low shelf fer hour un 'alf or 'til tender.

Where am yow agooen?

Now, think on. After all that fittlin' 'n drinken the Black Country con be a bit of a nightmare ter find yer way abahrt. One thing is that even us locals doe exactly know where it starts an finishes. This very issue can be the cause o many a pub debate!

Usually it is defined by the coal fields and the heavy industries it fuelled. There is however some guidance. We ay as north as Stafford an travelin south we definitely stop afower BRUM! Should you be in need of directions around the Black Country always try to find a local. They are easily spotted as the industrial stoop is usually an indicator. They will be friendly in the main if not a little suspicious or interested in why you want to go where you want to go. They might even want a chat before they offer you any indication of where you would like to go. This we say is gooin rarnd th'ouses, or not getting to the point. A little like this paragraph!

After asking for directions to your destination be prepared to be greeted with the immortal sentence 'If ar wuz you ar wouldn't 'ave started from ere. It'd a bin better if yowed come from th'other direction but waert a minute….'

After some time, head scrotchin' and turning round you will then hear 'Arn gorrit, waert a minute……well, yo con either goo right eyer, tek fust left, second right, straert on at the fust island, sharp left third right at the second island past th'ownd pub thet ay there anymower, past the metal foundry that they've terned into a museum of werk, then turn right, come back yerself a bit an yo cort miss it. Ooh 'ang on, yo cort goo that way now they'n changed ett all an added a buzz laerne, so what might be best is if yo turn ararned goo back along eyer an………'

Railways that criss-cross the region are called cuttings and canals are cuts. You can 'cut off' somewhere as in 'go away' so never try to make sense of 'cut off along the cut'. Streets are 'oss rowds' here so it can get worse. You can 'cut off along the cut but keep ahrt tho'ss rowd' Which is 'get out of my way but stay safe'! Now one person fell into the trap of trying to find Sandwell and Dudley train station. Dudley wuz allus sid as a posh town. It has a Zoo an Castle so how posh dun yo want ett? It also had a lot of heavy steel industries, glass industries and coal workings. Sandwell is the metropolitan

New motorway link, owd railway.
1960's transport priority unveiled!

borough of six industrialised towns, which include, Tipton, Wednesbury, West Bromwich, Oldbury, Smethwick, which were steeped in steel, coal, pottery, glass making and brick making industries, and Rowley (famous for roadstone and a high point (Rowley Rag) for grazing sheep). Dudley can easily be found on a map along with the constituent parts of Sandwell. But look for Sandwell and you'll struggle. So pity the poor individual who stopped a local in West Bromwich (home of 'Sandwell Valley Nature Reserve) saying they were looking for Sandwell and Dudley train station. They went on to say that they had been to Dudley and it wasn't there and now they couldn't find it in West Bromwich either, the place with a Sandwell reference. 'No! Nor yow woe find ett eyer or theyer cos it's in Owdbury!"

An 'istorical view of the Black Country mon an ooman at um an abroad

One thing the Black Country temperament is, is proud and loyal to itself an' it's own. Back in the times when life was much simpler families would often settle their differences in their own way shall we say. One such incidence was when a problem had arisen that required a conclusion ter be sought over a neighbourhood dispute. Each family went to its own end o the street armed with shovels, brooms or anything else that'd mek somebody squayel. They walked along wi the intention ter meet at the central point. Just like High Noon! Just on it tew squad cars appeared one either end o the street, obviously the coppers ad bin tipped off regarding the impending fracas. Just on it those who had been adversaries heard the police whistles and squad car bells and decided swift action needed to be taken. Suddenly they were protecting each other from the police by getting off the street and sheltering in each other's wums until the police had gone. The day eventually passed by peacefully and many new friendships were made!

Now if yo gerra map o the werld there ay many countries that Black Country folk ay touched either directly or indirectly. The industry from this little place went global whether it's raw materials for finishing right over to bridges and engineering. But if yo look on the map of North America yo'll see a lot o Black Country town naermes. Fer instance Tipton appears many times from the east coast ter the west coast. In fact there wuz a Tipton train robbery in the late nineteenth century in America! A lot of people went from the Black Country to find fame fortune or infamy! If you like, the Wild West Midlands went into the Wild West of America! It is rumoured that relatives of Wyatt Earp still live in the region such is the connection with that plaerce and period. One such story is set in Victorian times and is that of tew Black Country families who just dae gerron. Allus feudin they wuz so much so that one o the families decided they'd ad enough and decided ter uproot an goo to America. Ter saerve faerce the other family decided wot wuz gud fer that family wuz gud enough fer them an all. They all decided ter travel on the saerme day an when they got ter port they just so happened to be boarding the saerme ship. So all the way over the Atlantic they wuz arguing an carryin on. Now yo'd think that after a jerny like that they'd a tossed a coin when they got to America ter see oo went where. They day. They went to the east coast and carried on their feud right across the central states until they met the Pacific coast. Whether they ever

West Bromwich Albion supporters- other teams are available in
the area including Wolves and Walsall!

patched things up an become the best o naerbours we doe
know. One things fer sure, neither on em backed darn ter let
the other think they'd won the argument!

Gooin up in the werld (Stacks o' flats)

The housing stock in the region still contains miles and miles
of old spec built terraced houses, those beautifully
proportioned Victorian and Edwardian villas that give an
area a sense of being there forever. Not all housing stock was
like this. Throughout the depression years a lorra the owd
one up one down, back to backs and court properties were

demolished during slum clearancing. This gid way to more modern semi-detached properties being built through the inter- and post-war periods. This building programme also went into producing massive council estates for the more modern working family. In fact we had many pre-fabricated estates as well which were made of pre-formed concrete and asbestos. They tended to be hot in summer and cold in winter but as someone who lived in one these buildings once towd me, the rainstorms were fantastic! You could hear the rain on the tin roofs drumming away for hours and how they fell under the spell of that sound and rhythm when gooing ter sleep.

High spots un low uns

A further burst of housing for the masses came through the early to mid nineteen-sixties. Instead of putting people in rows somebody decided ter stack we in columns. This time it wasn't streets or estates it was tower blocks!

By the mid-sixties tower blocks were springing up all over the place. One group of flats near to Dudley had the reputation of being one of the coldest places to live in an urbanised landscape. No matter how much insulation or heating was applied to em it wuz still like living in an ice box. It wort until some bod in a warm office gorra map ahrt that they fun ahrt the wort no geographical feature tall enough ter stop the

Highrise living with a view to industry!

north easterly winds blowin directly from off the Ural Mountains in Russia!

As years passed and the newness of high-rise living wore off we tower block kids began to get somewhat of a reputation, deservedly or not. What had been sold as a concept of utopian living soon became, to some extent, a social housing nightmare. A tight knit community suddenly became scared to open their front dower cos o bad people being the other side on ett. There were some fun times and some scary moments though.

The courncil sed me mutha an faertha ad gorra move ahrt me gran's house cos it wuz deemed overcrowded wi six on we in a three bedroomed terrace with outdower lavvy. So I gid up me gardin as a fower year owd and the galvanised bath in front o the kitchen fire and had em replaced with a bathroom and a twelve foot be three foot balcony seven floors up instead! As I grew up I learned ter ride a bike in me bedroom an ow long a Scalextric track could be built until th'electric day reach the last hairpin bend!

All this modern stuff abart interior design wort needed in aer trendy flats either. As kids we could werk aert wot colours were on trend by the tins o paint bein set fire tew under visitors' cars. This happened on such a regular basis we ad aer own fire injin fer a while!

In me late teens though we had a real scare. We wuz woke up in the middle o the night ter the sound o we naerber abangin on aer front dower (well it couldn't a bin the back un cos it wuz undred foot off the floower!). We went ter open the dower an wuz met wi a wall o smoke so me an mutha gorrowd o the dog an wrapped in in wet towels an ad ter run darn fourteen flights o stairs to the great outdowers. That's when I realised ow fresh the air could smell even in the most polluted of atmospheres. It turned out that the fires on three landing were caused by electric distribution boards blowing an sendin fire dowers sprawling across the landings. The short circuits ad bin caused by rainwaerter gerrin in th'electrics. How, may you ask, did that happen? Some people oo owned dogs instead o walkin em on the graernd ter let their pooches do what dogs do had bin walkin em on the roof o the flats. The 'soil' as we'll call ett ad blocked the drains and the waerter had ter find anutha way in. So it did. We ad police and ambulances an when we wuz allowed back in ter we flats naerbers wi gas cookers med drinks fer them on we oo wuz all 'lectric and suddenly a sense of community was back together through a situation of adversity.

A lesson in culture

Me girlfriend (now me missus) is frum Wednesbury. Wednesbury was once seen as quite a posh town, a bit like Dudley, I mean it ad shaps! Well I wort let inter 'er 'ouse fer a bit when I fust started cootin 'er as 'er mom an dad eard I

Demolition of the 'cloud factory'

wuz frum Tipton. Such is the divide of a geographical mile! Well when I'd convinced 'er parents of my honourable intentions er stayed over at ma plaerce one night (in separate rooms of course!) and er woke up ter the industrial sunrise that greeted yer over the Seven Winds Steppin' Bridge (so-called cos it wuz allus windy an it used to be a bridge to a long gone and forgotten stretch o canal) ony ter see a bloke backin 'is tatter's oss (a horse for pulling scrap waggons and traps) aert o the graernd floor of a nearby maisonette. Such is the love we 'ave eya fer osses and their well-being!

Thanks fer thee cumpney

We may not have much in the way of obvious breath taking scenery here in the Black Country. You have to look for that around the ring roads and brown field sites. Our parks are still good green oases in the concrete and the clay. Our canals are very pretty and have gone through clean-ups and been made more accessible. We have fine industrialist and industrial architecture. We have history, tradition and pride that has been sweated for in some of the most dangerous and hostile conditions industry and its revolution could create. Go into the pubs and clubs hear the dialect and stories from the new generations of poets and musicians. Get a 'feel' for the area don't just see it. You can be assured of a warm welcome and huge meals! 'Navvy meals' as we call them here taken from the word navigation. This was a term given to all the workers who built and travelled the cuttings on waerter, road, n rail. We are passionate about our heritage and culture and we want others to share in it. In this post industrial landscape we have inherited a sense of humour as well as a sense of belonging to this region that is forged from industry and poverty. Those human qualities are is still very much in evidence today. Find 'em for theeselves.

Nah mine's a pint o' local brew if yo si me ahrt an abahrt burrin the meantime look after theeself n keep ahrt th'oss rowed!

Coal picking at Rowley

Dedicated to all those characters that make this region a great place to come from. Bostin aer kid!

ACKNOWLEDGEMENTS

A project of this magnitude relies entirely on its team, a group that fo[r] one month becomes inextricably bound by the destiny of this book. We would like to thank them individually for their time, effort, dedicatio[n] and tolerance. By name they are;

•**for their proof reading** - Matthew Boucher at the German Wine Information Service, Debbie Collinson, Patricia Coward, Justin Howard Sneyd, Willie Lebus at Bibendum, Chris Orr, Sue Pike at Wines of Chile Philip Reedman at the Australian Wine Club, Bella Thomas, Juli[a] Trustram Eve at the English Wine Producers and Anthony Whittaker o[f] Trout Wines

•**from WINE magazine** - Lorna Crosbie-Smith, Richard Davies, Ke[v] Daylami, Paul Flint, Robert Joseph, Charles Metcalfe, Damian Riley Smith, Alan Scott and Neil Singleton.

•**from the International WINE Challenge** - Sam Davies, Anthony Evans-Pughe, Sarah Fitch, Andrew Grant, Jack Lewens, Paul Phillipson Olivia Richmond, all the tasters who participated in the 199[5] International WINE Challenge, too numerous to list in this small guide and to all the other 40 Challenge helpers

•**for design, subbing and database management** - Jamie Ambrose Corinna Farrow, Renee Ferguson, Veronica Lyons, Peter Makin at Makin Rochard, Gavin Sailor, Simon Woods.

Special thanks to Frances Kiernan for her determination and energy She left no stone unturned in bringing this project to fruition.

HOW YOU CAN HELP US

If you have any ideas about how we can improve the format of the *WINE* Magazine Pocket Wine Buyer's Guide then please write to us at **652 Victoria Road, South Ruislip, Middlesex, HA4 0SX.**
The sort of subjects we would like to hear about are:-

•**Do you prefer to have countries subdivided by region or grape variety?**

•**Do you find the Under £5 guide at the back of the book useful?**

•**In what other ways would you like to see the wines subdivided?**

•**Do you require tasting notes in the book?**

•**Would you prefer the book to be loose leafed or ring bound like a filofax?**